DATE DUE

THE STORY OF
MONEY

CAROLYN KAIN

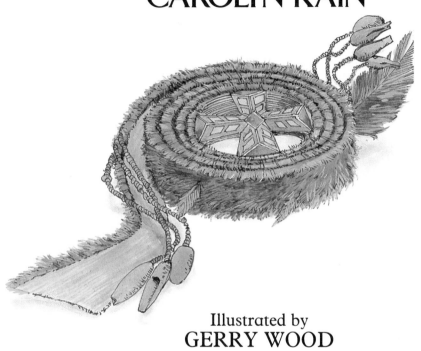

Illustrated by
GERRY WOOD

Troll Associates

Library of Congress Cataloging-in-Publication Data

Kain, Carolyn.
   The story of money / by Carolyn Kain; illustrated by Gerry Wood.
     p.   cm.
   Summary: Surveys the history of money, including both coins and
paper money, and explains how it functions in the world of today.
   ISBN 0-8167-2711-2 (lib. bdg.)   ISBN 0-8167-2712-0 (pbk.)
   1. Money—Juvenile literature. 2. Money—History—Juvenile
literature. [1. Money—History. 2. Money.] I. Wood, Gerald,
ill. II. Title.
HG231.K16 1993
332.4—dc20   91-38898

Published by Troll Associates

© 1994 Eagle Books

Design by James Marks
Edited by Kate Woodhouse

Printed in the U.S.A.

10 9 8 7 6 5 4 3 2 1

Contents

Exchange of goods

Long ago, people had to wander from place to place searching for food. But about 10,000 years ago, people found that if they collected seeds and planted them, a crop would grow. They also learned to tame wild animals. Now they had a permanent food supply and there was no need to wander. Gradually small villages grew up.

These people made baskets, sacks, and pots for storing their food. They also made tools to dig the land, harvest their crops, and build their homes. Over the years, they discovered that some people were better at making pots, while others were better at making baskets or hoes. The pot-maker might exchange a pot for some food, or a tool. Someone who made an ax might feel it was worth four pots, because the ax took longer to make. The people must have agreed upon a fair way of exchanging items.

▼ Once people settled in villages they developed new skills, such as making tools for digging the land and cutting the grain.

▲ It was in the Middle East, where the soil is rich and fertile, that people first grew crops.

5

The marketplace

People carefully chose the place where they settled. Villages often grew up where there was good soil for growing crops, or plenty of clay for making pots, or reeds for making baskets. As a result, some villages might have more grain than they needed or more pots than they needed. If the people could not trade goods within the village, they took them to a marketplace. Here people from several villages met to exchange their goods for items they needed. This system of trading is called barter. Often it works well, but sometimes there are problems, as in the following example.

◄ The people at this market are busy trying to find someone to barter with, but it is not always easy to find the right person.

Four people, each with something to barter, arrive at the marketplace. One has fish and wants a spear, another has a spear and needs grain, a third has grain and would like a pot, and the fourth has a pot but wants a spear. Unfortunately, no one gets anything.

7

Precious objects

It became obvious that a system of exchange does not always work, so people in different parts of the world developed ways of solving this problem. Certain objects were agreed upon as being precious. If you sold something, you received a number of these objects. If you then wanted to buy something, you would pay with them. These objects were used as money.

In some Pacific Islands, people used stone wheels for buying and selling goods. Cattle, tools, weapons, packets of salt, cacao beans, glass beads, and bricks of pressed tea have all been used as money. In parts of Africa, people used cowrie shells. But when traders arrived from India, they would not sell their goods for cowrie-shell money. In India thousands of these shells were washed up on the beaches, so to the Indians this kind of money was worthless.

► Some types of early money, like cattle, tools, weapons, and salt packets, were useful in themselves. Other items like cowrie shells, glass beads, and Yap stones, were used as tokens in buying and selling, just as money is used today.

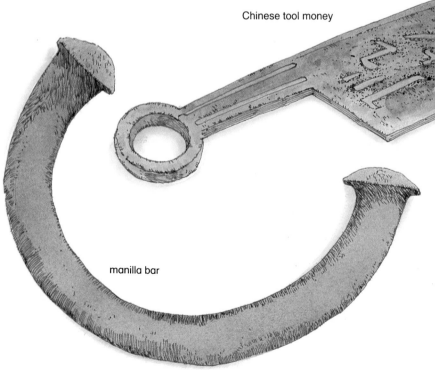

Yap stone

Chinese tool money

manilla bar

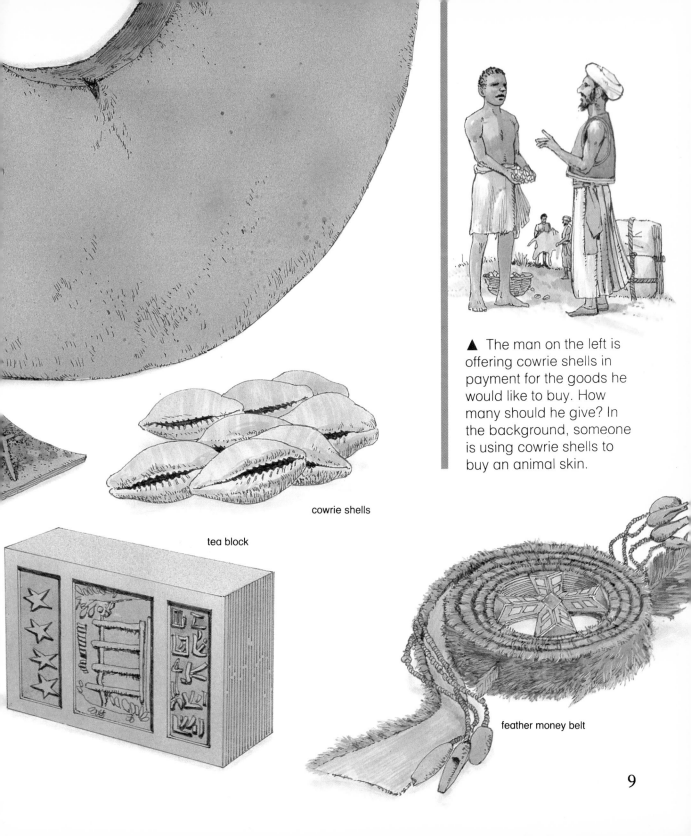

▲ The man on the left is offering cowrie shells in payment for the goods he would like to buy. How many should he give? In the background, someone is using cowrie shells to buy an animal skin.

cowrie shells

tea block

feather money belt

9

The first coins

As trade in different parts of the world increased, it became necessary to find something that was precious to everyone. Gold and other rare metals were already valued for their beauty. In Babylon, chips from gold and silver bars were weighed and used as money. In Egypt, gold and silver bands were weighed on scales using stone or bronze weights in the shapes of animals. These animals had formerly been used as money. The first coins were made about 2,700 years ago.

▼ Traders visited Babylon with precious, perfumed oils to sell. This wealthy merchant paid for the oils with gold pieces, chipped from a bar of solid gold.

► This Egyptian used scales to balance bands of gold and silver against a stone shaped as an ox.

In China, the first coins were called cash. In Greece, each small coin was marked with its weight. Later, important gods and rulers were pictured on the coins. Roman bronze coins pictured a cow. This reminded people that coins were valuable in the same way as cattle.

▲ This "owl" coin comes from Athens. The owl was a special bird of the goddess Athena. The Athenians used this coin for trading with their neighbors, many of whom liked the design so much that they used it on their own coins.

▲ The use of a king's head on coins is over two thousand years old. This coin shows Antiochus III of Syria.

▲ A silver "stater," a coin that came from Corinth in Greece dating from the 5th century B.C.

11

Minting coins

Coins were both convenient and durable. As the demand for them increased, it became necessary to set up coin factories. These factories were called mints. They had to be secure, and the people working in them had to be honest. Monasteries were often used as mints.

At first the coins were made by hand. Raw metal was heated until it melted. It was then poured out to form sheets. When the sheets were cool, they were cut into blank shapes, each of the same weight. The blank was then put between two dies, each marked with a picture. The dies were struck together so that the picture was pressed onto each side. Making each coin was a slow process. About 300 years ago, machines were developed that could quickly produce large quantities of coins.

sovereign

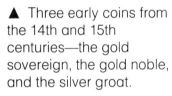

noble

groat

▲ Three early coins from the 14th and 15th centuries—the gold sovereign, the gold noble, and the silver groat.

◄ The people in this mint are making coins by hand. When the coins were made, they went to be weighed and counted by the owner of the mint.

13

Countries without money

In Europe and Asia, trade and the use of money changed the everyday lives of most people. But there were places where money was not used.

In Peru, there was plenty of gold, but it was not used to make coins. Instead, the people made magnificent ornaments and decorations for their temples. The ruler of this land was called the Inca. His people were not paid to work. Each person did their fair share of work for the good of everyone.

Almost 500 years ago, Francisco Pizarro and an army of Spanish soldiers went to Peru. Pizarro did not want to trade but to conquer the Inca and his land. Pizarro imprisoned the Inca, defeated his army, and took many of the people as slaves. The people's gold, stripped from their beautiful temples, was shipped back to Spain to be melted down and made into coins.

▼ The Inca told Pizarro that he would fill one room with gold and two others with silver in exchange for his freedom. Pizarro was not interested in this offer.

▲ In Mexico, the Aztecs did not use money either. This shield, together with a warrior's costume, was worth 64 cloaks.

15

Lawbreakers

Year after year, more gold and silver were taken by the Spanish from South America. The voyage back to Spain was never easy, because Dutch, French, and English ships often lay in wait to seize the treasure on these ships. There were many pirates at sea and highwaymen on land who were willing to take great risks to make their fortune.

Others broke the law by clipping pieces of gold and silver from the edges of coins. It was difficult to tell whether a coin had been clipped, until mints began to mill the edges of coins with tiny ridges.

Many rulers tried to save their gold and silver. They started to make their coins with a mixture of cheaper metals. This meant the coins were no longer worth their weight in gold or silver, but they were still used as tokens for buying and selling goods.

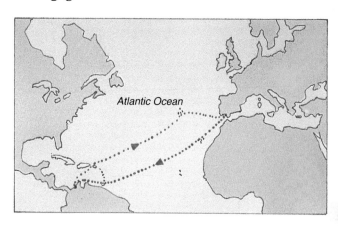

▲ This map shows one of the routes taken by treasure ships from South America to Europe.

▲ ▼ In England, pennies were marked with a long cross so that it was easier to see if they had been clipped. But it was only when coins were milled that it became impossible to cut the edge off a coin unnoticed.

Paper money

In London, wealthy people needed safe places to store large amounts of money. Goldsmiths, who made jewelry, had strong rooms in their shops. They often locked away other people's money and valuables for safekeeping, and gave them a written receipt in return. This receipt could then be used to buy something. Goldsmiths were like the banks of today, and their receipts were England's first paper money.

Soon banks were set up especially to provide these security services. The banks each held a supply of gold. Each bank note promised to pay the person who brought it to the bank a certain amount of gold.

Early bank notes were easy to copy. Banks soon decided to number each note and print them with intricate patterns that were hard to copy. Today, bank notes have a watermark and a metal strip to make them more difficult to forge.

► This rich London lady has brought her money to be stored safely by the goldsmith. He gives her a written receipt. When she wants the money back, she will hand over the receipt. The receipt is a kind of paper money.

▲ The Chinese invented paper money more than 4,000 years ago. It was printed with blue ink on paper made from the mulberry tree.

▲ Today, special paper containing a watermark and metal strip, intricate patterns, and serial numbers make paper money difficult to copy.

19

Money in the bank

Today people are encouraged to save their money. When you deposit your money in a bank, you earn money, called interest. The bank lends your money to people who need to borrow. They have to pay this money back and give the bank interest. The bank makes sure that it receives more interest from borrowers than it gives to savers, so it can make money for itself.

Banks offer many other services. A person's wages can be paid directly into a bank account. The account holder can spend this money by taking cash from the bank or by writing checks, which give the bank permission to pay out money to someone else. Account holders can ask for a statement at any time, which will show exactly how much money is in their account. The bank will quickly let the account holders know if they have spent more money than they have in their account!

► Most people keep their money in a bank account. When you go into a bank, you will see many people serving customers at the counter. There are many other people who work there, keeping accounts of the money handled by the bank and advising people on money matters.

Business and profit

▼ A factory making wooden toys must earn money to buy more wood, maintain its buildings and machines, and pay its workers. It must also pay for the cost of transporting the toys to shops. These costs are the factory's overhead.

Every business wants us to buy its goods or services, so it can earn money. Some of this money is used to run the business. These costs are called overhead. All of these costs are paid for by the customers in the price of what they buy. If the business cannot pay for its overhead, it will close and the workers will become unemployed.

▼ The shop that buys the toys has a number of costs itself, so it must earn money on the sale of the toys to customers.

Some businesses are owned by one person. Any money left over after the overhead has been paid belongs to that person and is called profit. Other businesses are owned by people who are shareholders. Each shareholder has bought a part, or share, of the business and receives a share of the profits. Sometimes the profit goes back into the business so that it can expand.

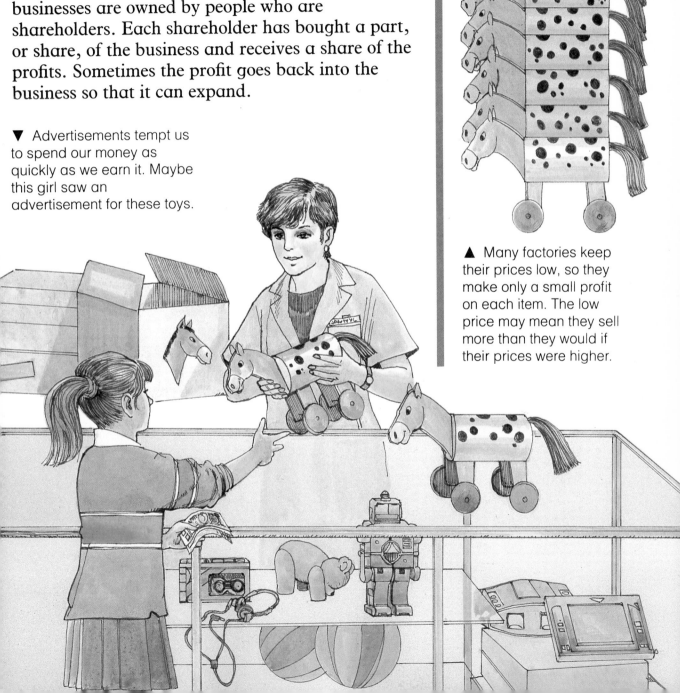

▼ Advertisements tempt us to spend our money as quickly as we earn it. Maybe this girl saw an advertisement for these toys.

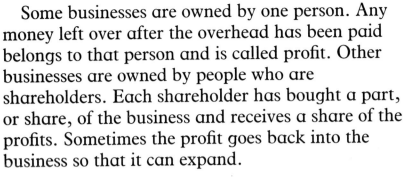

▲ Many factories keep their prices low, so they make only a small profit on each item. The low price may mean they sell more than they would if their prices were higher.

Making and sharing money

As people earn money, they have to pay some of it to the government in tax. Taxes are used to benefit everyone. Taxes pay for schools, roads, the police, and the country's defense. Some of the money is used to pay retired workers, the unemployed, disabled people, and others who do not have enough money of their own.

The more people earn, the more they are supposed to pay in taxes. In this way the government tries to make sure that everyone pays his or her fair share of the country's expenses.

▼ This man is building a factory, which will create new jobs. If he makes profits, he may get rich. He and his workers will pay taxes. These will be used to benefit everyone.

▼ This man is borrowing money for a new car. He agrees to pay interest on the money borrowed. If he cannot repay the loan, the bank can take the car and sell it to recover the money they have loaned.

▲ A pawnbroker's sign. People sometimes take an item of value to the pawnbroker. He gives them money for it and keeps it until they can buy it back.

Rich and poor

In the richer countries, like those of Europe and
North America, few people die of hunger. But in
poorer countries this happens all too often. These
countries have little of value to sell to other
countries. So their governments have little money.
They must rely on their people to grow their own
food because they cannot afford to buy it from
other countries. If there is no rain and the crops
fail, the people have no food. Then some of the
richer countries help by providing aid. But much
more help is needed so that these countries can find
reliable ways of feeding themselves.

Meanwhile, the richer countries have large quantities of crops and other valuables to sell. Anything they do not have themselves, they can afford to buy from other countries.

▼ This truck is bringing food to these hungry people. Money can always help, but it must be used wisely. It might be well spent on teaching new farming methods, building a dam, or planting trees.

The future

The way money will be used in the richer countries is bound to change in the future. Plastic cards are safe and convenient, so they may replace the need for cash and checks. Home computers will be linked to banks so that we can have immediate information on our bank accounts. They may also be linked to shops, so we can see and choose the items we want to buy on our computer screens.

It is also possible that, instead of each country having its own currency, there will be one currency for the whole world. Already countries that belong to the European Community are planning a common currency called the *ecu*.

People have used many kinds of currency through the ages. But no matter what kind of money we use, it is only by spending it wisely that its real value can be measured.

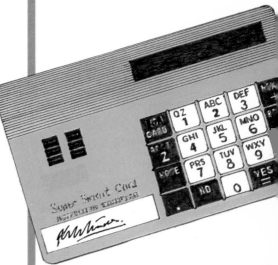

▼ People with their own terminals will be able to deal with all their money matters from home. It will probably be many years before every home is as well equipped as this one.

▲ A smart card. This may be one of the pocket machines of the future. It is a combination of a plastic credit card and a computer which can make payments in different currencies. It may not prove useful, but other types of cards may be developed from this idea. Who knows what they will be like?

Fact file

Currency

The money that is used in a particular country is its currency: the United States of America uses the dollar and cent; Japan has the yen; Britain has the pound and penny; and Mexico has the peso and centavo. Each country has its own currency. When you go abroad you may have to change your money into the currency of the country you are visiting.

Aid

Aid is the word used to describe the money, food, and other help given by a richer country to a poorer one. Sport Aid in 1986 was the biggest-ever event to raise funds for aid. It raised over $110 million, with 20 million people running in 78 countries and 277 cities all over the world.

▶ Many people collect old coins. This hobby is called numismatics. Coins are sometimes worth several hundred times more than their original value if they are very old and rare. Coins that are found in the remains of old buildings can tell us something of the past. Coins found in Roman remains, for example, often have the head of the emperor, his name, and the date stamped on them.

Roman

Portuguese

American

Greek

Dies

Dies are the metal shapes with raised patterns that are used for printing paper money or stamping coins.

Metal in coins

Although coins were originally made from pure gold and silver, they are now made from a mixture of cheaper metals. These mixtures are called alloys.

Brown coins were originally made from copper. Tin and zinc often were added to the copper to make it harder. American pennies are copper-coated zinc.

Silver coins are usually made from copper and nickel. Nickel is a hard-wearing metal that makes the coin look silver.

▼ Ancient Chinese "cash" is still being issued today. The hole is so that people can wear these coins on a string around their neck.

silver thaler

American dollar

◄ ► In the 16th century large, silver coins were issued called "thalers." They were named after Joachimsthal, the town in the Austro-Hungarian empire where the silver was mined. The English word "dollar" has developed from thaler.

Index